Based

The Day I Gave Jesus a Bologna Sandwich

James Bunch

Table of Contents

Dedication

This book is dedicated to my brother, Samuel, who died at a young age due to a farming accident in the early 1970s. You never got a chance to experience graduating from high school or college. You never knew what it was like to fall madly in love or get married and have children of your own. You never got the opportunity to buy your first new car, take an airline flight, or even see an ocean.

Everything good I do in life I do just a little extra for you. See you in paradise, bro!

CHAPTER 1

Jesus, Me, and the U.S. Fish and Wildlife Service

Here's what you need to know upfront. I'm a Christian and country boy. I'm blessed to be a sixty-two-year-old African American male. I stress the word *blessed*! Why? Because like many of you I've traveled a rocky road, and in some cases a most un-holy one at that.

I grew up on a small farm in a little place called Becton, Arkansas. Becton is located approximately six miles north of another small town called Cotton Plant. To say the least, both towns were rural, so we made our living working the rice, cotton, and soybean fields. In most cases these fields were owned by white farmers.

I can vividly recall the lowest rate of pay I ever received after toiling all day in a cotton field. Six dollars. Yep, that's it. This was my life and most of my cousins' and friends' lives during the late fifties through the mid-seventies. But it was a common way of life and it kept food on our tables. We knew no other way of doing things.

But through God's Grace this part of my life became an integral part of the presentations I would occasionally give to young people when I promoted careers in agriculture.

My parents, Jewell B and Addie Lee Bunch, had a total of seventeen children. Three girls and fourteen boys. Needless to say, and if it wasn't already clear, we were poor. It was later in life that I learned why my parents and other married couples in the community had so many children. I know you must be curious about this, too, so let me enlighten you. Back in those times, after the Great Depression and pre-Civil Rights, if you were poor and lived in a rural community, it was necessary to have a large family. You see, we were farm laborers. If you were one of the few and far in between, a family that owned a significant amount of land, you needed free labor because machinery was expensive. And if in the more likely scenario you lived on land owned by a white farmer, your chances of staying in his sharecropper house were increased if you had enough kids to work his crops.

*****

So, what's this book about? Well, what I would like for you to do as the reader is to think back over your life and consider that there's a good chance that James Bunch's story is your story. Let me be more specific. As unique as each one of us is here on planet Earth, there is one thing for certain: there is only one God.

But let me say a little more about this book. It's about my personal journey with race relations here in America; coming of age during the sixties, seventies, and eighties; and, last but not least, God's Grace and Jesus's

Providence. You will notice that in each of the chapters in this book I place my Friend Jesus front and center, then I talk about agriculture. Why? Of course, we would not be here if not for his willingness to bear the cross for us, and, well, agriculture is a necessity for life. There's a connection between these two things that I hope you will see.

Even though my story is just one among the millions of stories all of us have lived, it's important to remember that we're all individuals, we're distinctive, just like the paths we follow to find Jesus and the ways he impacts us individually. I was a sinner, a wretch undone. But I don't just believe this, I also know for certain that on many occasions Jesus saved me.

Growing up with all those brothers and sisters was exciting! Although our financial resources were limited there was an abundance of love. And what our parents taught us would help the road we each travelled in life be a lot smoother. To date none of us have ever experienced what it's like to look out of a jail cell, but we looked in on them when visiting relatives and friends. Our parents did not receive a high school diploma or a college degree, but they believed in higher education and guided most of us to graduate from high school. And many of us received college degrees.

As I reminiscence, one key thing I recall about my parents during the turbulent times of the sixties is that they were always calm. All I have to do is consider how we and other black families were living and how the white families were living. I am certain there was some resentment based on how life was during this period. Perhaps our parents felt this resentment as well, but they never revealed it. Instead they taught us to be mindful of our place and to be respectful. I thank God they had that sense. Little did I know they were preparing us not to be accepted and loved by our white brothers and sisters but by Jesus Christ.

I vividly recall the night of the assassination of Dr. Martin Luther King, Jr. in Memphis, Tennessee, while watching our grainy black and white television set. I heard no swearing or racial slurs about our white brothers and sisters. In fact, I never once heard my parents say a negative word about whites in general. We were taught to treat our white employers, the local farmers, with respect and to work hard for them. Sometimes I didn't understand why we had to live the way we did, why, that is, we had to work so hard for so little money.

Although we had limited financial resources, our home was full of love. In fact, it was a joy to eat food that was grown by our hands. Back then gardening was a necessity. We practiced "locally grown," "know your farmer, know your food," long before it became trendy. It was "farm to table" every day for us. Moreover, we were vegetarians and did not know it. I can recall many days of having a meal with no meat. It was normal. I was a skinny kid like many of my siblings and other youth in the community.

But even though I was skinny and hungry most of the time, I had a skill that God chose to give to me: I was fast as a jack rabbit. I did not know this initially, but here's how I found out.

My brother, Theodis, came home from school one day and I heard him say he was running track. That sounded like a lot of hard work, something that was not for me. But the more he went to practice, the more I begin to notice something important. Practice was after school. This meant he did not have to do any of the chores around our small farm because we would finish them before he got home. That's when the light bulb went on in my head!

So, one day I approached my parents and asked if I could also run track. Looking at me standing there, not even ninety pounds soaking wet, they both said no. "You might get hurt," they said. I didn't know anything about track and field, so I didn't have a counterargument. But I asked my brother, "Hey, what's involved in track and field? And what do you do?" His reply was straightforward.

"All you do is run. Just be faster than the next guy."

I went back and convinced my parents that because it's just running there is no way I could get hurt. So that's what I did: I ran. And as I was blessed by God, I was fast. In fact, I was so fast I got a full scholarship to the University of Arkansas at Pine Bluff (UAPB). So long cotton fields!

*****

In the Fall of 1975, I landed on the Yard at UAPB in Pine Bluff. It was fantastic. For once I had my own bunk bed! Also, I only had to share the bedroom with one person. But that was weird in another way. He was my track teammate, and he was Jamaican and from New York

City. It took me a while to understand him as his dialect was something I had never experienced. I remember being very cautious, because all he talked about was having sex with numerous girls. As time progressed, we slowly bonded and he was the first person to introduce me to reggae music and the great Bob Marley and the Whalers. I've been a fan ever since.

Being on campus was exciting! My home boys and I met young people from other small rural towns just like ours. We all had similar socioeconomic backgrounds. We all worked on the farms for the local white landowners. With this background, choosing a major came easy. It would be agriculture. Agronomy, to be exact. It was a breeze. Even though I struggled with math and a few other subjects, I did well overall in my classes.

I proudly wore the mantle of being a country boy. One of my teammates, Jack from New Orleans, would quip by saying "Bunch, I can tell just by watching as guys walked across campus whether they are a country boy or city boy."

I say, "How?"

He goes, "A city boy looks up when he's walking in order not to be flattened by a car if he misses a traffic light. On the other hand, a country boy looks down to make certain he does not step on a snake or other poisonous critter that could kill him."

A simple matter of survival for each. Needless to say, this particular teammate was a jive turkey.

While away from home, I would lie awake many nights thinking about our place in the country and wonder what my life would be like moving forward. Now that I was free (I guess you could call it that) I did not have to get up and go to church on Sunday mornings. But I never forgot those walks and the sermons and just the gathering of everyone from the community.

Track and field in college was at a whole other level than high school. I was now facing guys who had the drive and intensity I did, so I had to get used to losing. But it was exciting to travel to different states and universities. It was great to meet young folks from other rural communities as well as from cities Chicago, New York, Memphis, New Orleans, and many others.

I enjoyed listening to the upperclassmen brag about their exploits on and off the field as we travelled between meets. My freshman year was so-so. I didn't have many wins as an individual runner (440-yard dash) or running a leg on the mile relay (4X440). However, my status as a trackster changed the last track meet of the season. During the final race of the 440-yard dash, from out of nowhere I got this enormous burst of energy and demolished the field, which included my senior teammate. Immediately after the race our coach came over and congratulated me and told me that for the first time, I had broken fifty seconds and that moving forward I would be his quarter miler! It was at that moment I considered myself a real track star!

What a great life I was having attending UAPB. I tell you there is nothing like the experience of going to an Historically Black College and University (HBCU). Our instructors loved and pushed us, helping us along the path to success. Although we had a few instructors that were of different ethnic backgrounds, for the most part my instructors were African American. But then again my hometown I grew up in was predominantly African American, all the people I worked in the cotton fields with were African American, and all the local towns we visited for sports were full of African Americans. Therefore, my next adventure in this life journey would totally shock me and open my eyes.

As I mentioned earlier, our parents never taught us to hate white people. As close as possible they followed the

Good Book and instilled in us to do the same. This discipline would prove to be invaluable to me in the summer of 1976.

*****

After having a great Freshman year at UAPB, I was off to my first job assignment. Where was I headed? To Chicago, New York, L.A. or New Orleans? No, I ended up in Ortonville, Minnesota. Where the heck is that? Since I was majoring in agriculture, I should have expected to end up in some little country town. I was given the great opportunity to work for the U.S. Fish and Wildlife Service that summer. One thing I knew for sure, though, is that I would not be chopping cotton this summer like so many of my friends and relatives back in Cotton Plant, so lets' go.

Here is a question I have for just my African American readers: When was the first time you truly realized that African Americans did not live everywhere in these great states? For the first eighteen years of my short life up to that point, I assumed that we were everywhere across these great states. That was my viewpoint, literally.

That summer I boarded the Greyhound bus at Pine Bluff. I was nervous and excited. I love going to new places and meeting new people. On the bus with me that morning there were a few African Americans. Our very first stop was Little Rock, where even more boarded. I thought "man, this is great. I can't wait to get to Ortonville, MN, and socialize with the African Americans who live there. It will be great to explore their culture." I even wondered if they ate the same foods as their southern brothers and sisters.

From Arkansas we travelled into Kansas. I noticed that most of the bus emptied as we proceeded to Iowa. When we pulled into Sioux City and I peered out the window, I saw a ton of folks getting ready to board. But there were no African Americans! Immediately the bus was eighty percent White. I'm thinking, "What is this? Perhaps at the next stop this will change."

The next major stop was the Twin Cities of Minneapolis and St. Paul. Those white passengers were replaced by other white passengers and one biracial female. Oops! The feeling of going to Minnesota and learning about the culture of other African Americans suddenly became dim. I mean this prospect was over in a flash. That young biracial female I just mentioned got off on the very next stop. Now it was just me. And I couldn't help noticing a lot of people were watching my every move. "Where the heck am I going?' I wondered.

Finally, the driver announced my stop. Ortonville! I got off and grabbed my bag. I looked north, I looked south, then east and west; I looked all around for an African American face, any face; old, young, male, female, I just wanted to see one.

I was sorely disappointed. There were a lot of eyes looking in amazement at me as well. These were white faces. And the look on their faces was like they assumed I had caught the wrong bus. Then suddenly out of the crowd came a middle-aged gentleman with his hand extended for a handshake. He said, "Hi, I'm Chuck. You must be James Bunch?"

Immediately my fears were calmed.

"Yes," I said, "that's me.

"You must be tired from such a long trip."

Then he said, "Let me grab your bags."

He did and asked if he could take me to the local hotel.

"Sure," I said, and we were off.

The following Monday morning I met the staff. Including Chuck, it was four white guys. Later that month we would be joined by an additional two white guys and two white women, each on a summer job like myself. There

I was, the center of attention. Everyone was cool and wanted to learn as much about me as they possibly could.

Except for this one guy named Butch.

Butch was very standoffish. I couldn't quite figure him out. He was middle aged, married with kids, and lived out in the country. In addition to his government job, he was a farmer. He raised sheep.

Keep in mind, I was used to working *for* white people, not *with* white people. That is, back in Arkansas the boss would pick us up in his pick-up truck, carry us to the field he wanted chopped or where he wanted the cotton picked, and then take us back home. So, I never imagined working in an office setting with whites. At least not by myself.

This was interesting. Initially, they seemed amused that I could hold an intelligent conversation. And yes, they admitted that all they ever saw and heard about African Americans was on the news and involved crime in the Twin

Cities. Coming from where I came, the whites and African Americans did not hold conversation. It was more like you were given an order and you carried out that order. We did not mix.

But back to Butch. After several days of his seemingly raw attitude toward me, I had the opportunity to confront him. This is the Addie Lee Bunch side of me. I recall it vividly. We were riding along one day and after a while he started quizzing me about my pay. Now, I know why Butch was mad at me. I came to find out I was making more than he was, and me just a sophomore in college (soon to be anyway). Well, I'm thinking that's got nothing to do with me. So, I let him have it. No, we did not go fisticuffs, I just explained to him that my education required that I'm compensated at a certain rate and that it was really none of his business what I was paid. After he saw that I wouldn't abide his attitude, things started to change. In fact, we started to get along pretty good. More on that later.

I could not afford the hotel rates I initially moved into, so I sought a more suitable and reasonable place to live. Chuck introduced me to a nice middle-aged white lady who was married with kids and whose husband was a truck driver and was rarely home. I thought surely this lady is not going to let me move in with her and her kids, and what would this guy say? But I came to find out they had a huge house with an apartment connected on the side. And yes, there I was living with a white family. Oddly, I never met her husband. I met her mom and dad, but the husband, no. Looking back on it now, I wonder whether she even had a husband. Perhaps this was just a cover. Anyhow, goodbye dumpy motel.

Here is where my story gets interesting as it relates to leaning on Jesus.

We've all heard the phrase *the coldest winter I ever spent was the summer I spent in San Francisco.* Well, the loneliest summer I ever spent was the summer I spent in Ortonville.

I was beginning to get over the shock of being the only African American in town, and the office atmosphere was great. I loved the work but after hours was when the loneliness set in. The apartment I lived in did not have a phone or television. At least the motel had girly magazines I could sneak a peek at when the manager wasn't looking. However, when my mom picked me up from my dorm and took me to the bus station, in her wisdom she handed me a Bible and said, "Take this with you."

Keep in mind, my suitcase was already stuffed with my clothes and other belongings, and although I had been eating three square meals a day with meat, I still only weighed 155lbs because every ounce I gained the track coach worked them off. Therefore, I told my mom thanks but there was no more room for the Bible. She gave me the look of "boy don't make me have to smack you in front of all these people in this bus station." So, I took the Bible and barely made room for it. I mumbled. I was sure I would never open it.

My first night lying there alone in that bed I thought about all my friends back home and how I wished I could just call and have a conversation. All the lights were out; it was completely silent. Then, suddenly, the bed began to violently shake! I thought there must be an intruder. I jumped up, prepared to fight. With what, my hands? I had no weapon. I flipped on the light switch and saw no one. I thought this was weird. Maybe I should run outside! But then reality got hold of me. Really, a young African-American running outside half naked in this town? That wasn't an option. So, I slowly bent over and looked under the bed. It was clear. Think, James Bunch, think. Then it hit me.

Perhaps this is not an evil spirit or something or someone wanting to do me harm. Perhaps this was just a hello from Jesus letting me know I am not alone. "I'm with you," he's saying. So, I switched off the light and laid back down and went calmly to sleep.

For the entire summer I never bought an alarm clock. Yet, I was never late for work.

The camaraderie between me and my white coworkers grew as the summer passed. July 4, 1976 wasn't only my 19th birthday, it was also America's 200th birthday. During the celebration I visited the hometown of two of my coworkers and we went canoeing on the great Mississippi River and did some rock climbing. This was the first time I was invited to stay at the home of a white American. Learning of my birthday prior to my visit, his parents even gave me a birthday card. In addition to the lovely words of congratulations, inside there was a twenty-dollar bill. This was very emotional and significant to me because this was the first time I received money from a white American and did not have to labor for it. As a country boy from the deep south, this was all new to me.

Wrapping up my summer job, the trust between Butch and I was so great that when he and his family went on vacation that summer, he wanted to pay me to house sit for him. I did it for free. And that Bible my mom gave me? I read it word for word. During that summer I was invited several times to the homes of my white brothers and sisters to share a meal, I was invited on vacation, and I was even loaned a television set. These simple acts of human kindness would forever change my impression of my relationship with my white brothers and sisters.

Memories of a Track Star: Part I

ALL-SPORTS

BANQUET

UNIVERSITY of ARKANSAS
at PINE BLUFF

STUDENT UNION LOUNGE

MAY 1, 1979

7:30 P.M.

UNIVERSITY OF ARKANSAS AT PINE BLUFF
1979 TRACK SCHEDULE

Date	Opponent	Place
March 9, 1979	Pre-AIC Relays	Hot Springs, AR
17	Arkansas Relays	Russellville, AR
24	Open	
31	Delta State Invitational	Cleveland, MS
April 7	Ouachita Baptist University Relays	Arkadelphia, AR
14	ASU Track Classic	Jonesboro, AR
19-20-21	Kansas Relays	Lawrence, KS
28	Mississippi Valley State Relays	Itta Bena, MS
May 5	Northeast Invitational	Monroe, LA
12	Open	
17-18-19	NAIA Outdoor Championship	Abeline, TX

Grant's Golden Lions Are NAIA Bound Again

Bob Christ
Of The Commercial Staff

Coach U.S. (Bubba) Grant and his University of Arkansas at Pine Bluff track team are a familiar sight at the National Association of Intercollegiate Athletics track and field national championships.

In the first five of his 12 years as head coach at UA-PB, Grant guided such All-America performers as Harold Francis, who holds the NAIA record in the 400-meter dash (45.6) to Aaron Harris's 9.4 100-yard dash. Then there was Alex Jackson, who went 50½ feet in the triple jump, which is still a state record, and Lars Allen, who gained his honors in the long jump (25.6). There was also Earl Goldman, who had a 1:48.5 in an 800-meter final ... and so on.

This season the entire Golden Lion team will be taking a trek to Abilene, Texas, for the next weekend's nationals. All five of them. No need in chartering a bus. They'll all fit comfortably in a school van. They'll sit at one table in restaurants. They'll share the same room. A real compact team.

Grant started the season with 22 track and field participants, but attrition took its toll, along with a 30-percent budget reduction as part of a school-wide cutback of spring sports. Without scholarships to earn, the sacrifice of running in Grant's program was perhaps too great for some.

Instead of calling it quits, however, and permitting the program he helped build to disintegrate, he molded the remaining talent into one of the finest squads in the nation.

"I sat down and looked at it (the roster) and said 'What can I do with five folks? If I have them run in all the events they'll be dead by April 1. What could be done to benefit the university most and benefit them?'" Grant asked.

So he sat down with the five — James Busch of Cotton Plant, Billy Farmer of Dermott, Elvis Paul of Franklin, Louisiana, and Herman Carter of Pine Bluff, all of whom are seniors, along along with a sophomore, Larry Coleman of Brinkley — and discussed the coming season.

They all were prepared to sacrifice.

Paul, an All-America long and triple jumper, all but ignored his specialties this season after qualifying for the finals in his usual meet, and disregarded training for the 100-meter dash to devote his energies toward running a leg on the mile relay team.

Coleman cast aside his hurdling aspirations and also diverted his efforts toward running the 440 as a part of the mile relay.

Busch and Farmer were already specialists in the event, so it was a natural that there would be a mile relay team and a darn good one. There would also be a sprint medley team, and in addition, Busch and Farmer would run open quarters. That was it.

"We've set (nine) meet records at everywhere we've been except the Kansas Relays," Grant said. "They appreciate sacrificing now. They get to travel (Texas Relays, Mississippi Valley State University Relays, Arkansas State Track Classic in Jonesboro). They've won seven team awards and any number of tee-shirts and gold watches all across the country."

In fact, two weeks ago at the MVSU meet in Itta Bena, Mississippi, Busch eclipsed the school meet (and state record in the 400 meters with a dash of 45.4. It bettered Francis's mark set in 1968.

Their success all started with dedication.

"There could be 15 inches of snow on the ground, but I told them that they should still think to come to practice," Grant said. "We'll sing the school song if we have to."

"I was going to go with one (athlete) if I had to," Grant added. "We were not going to go without a track program. You can never shut it down. It's too hard to start back up."

The competition for the mile relay will be fierce, according to Grant.

This year NAIA track schools are running better than in the past five years," he said. "Prairie View has run a 3:06.9, Southern of Baton Rouge has a 3:09.5 and Texas Southern has gone 3:10.7. We're capable of going 3:08 any day."

So far they've dropped to 3:08.0.

The backbone of the group is Busch, who anchors the mile relay. And ironically, Busch was not a highly recruited quartermiler.

"His times weren't that great," Grant said. "But I took him because his coach said he was a heckuva student and a hard worker."

From a 50.2 best at Cotton Plant he achieved All-America status as a freshman in the 400 meters with a 46.7 timing in the final while finishing sixth. Two years ago he took fourth with a 46.6. Last year he was third with a 46.6. He was also ranked first in the state — as he is this year.

"I've got to see something in a kid that hasn't come out yet," Grant said of his effort to survive recruiting wars. "And when I get a kid like that, I work twice as hard with him."

"That's the price of dedication."

JAMES BUSCH

Lions Break Mile Record

Special to The Commercial

MONROE, Louisiana — The University of Arkansas at Pine Bluff track team broke a Louisiana Festival of Champions track record in the mile relay here last night with a clocking of 3:09.0.

The four-man group of Billy Farmer (47.4), Elvis Paul (46.7), Larry Coleman (48.8) and James Bunch (46.5) eclipsed the mark of 3:10.7 set last year by Northeast Louisiana University.

The Lions' Bunch also won the 400 meters with a time of 46.6 while Farmer came in third with a 48.8.

"This will give us a good send-off for the (National Association of Intercollegiate Athletics) finals in Abeline," said UA-PB Track Coach U.S. (Bubba) Grant of the national meet which begins May 18. "We've finally been able to break the 3:10 barrier."

CHAPTER 2

Jesus, Me, and Mary Jane (Marijuana)

I'm now back on campus starting the Fall semester. My classmates and I swapped stories of our summer adventures. They were all similar. We had a good laugh about this new awakening about our country, one that we never knew existed.

It was back to my books and track and field. I'm no longer just a green freshman teammate. I have become the guy to beat, not only at UAPB but also the track circuit in which we participated. My wins started to rack up, especially in the individual 440-yard dash. The mile relay on the other hand was a different story. I now took the place as the anchor for the group replacing the senior that I beat the previous Spring.

My name began to appear in the local paper, the *Pine Bluff Commercial Appeal*, more frequently. I was enjoying the small celebrity status. And as far as classwork, I got my system down, including how to cram for exams the night before. But here I was blessed by God in another way. I was able to retain information I had studied just long enough to take the exam. Less than an hour after I had turned in my exam, it would leave my memory. And this was cool, I thought, because silly me believed I would never have to use this information ever again. Boy was I wrong.

But time flew by and before I knew it was the Spring of 1977, and I was expecting my new summer job assignment. Where would I be heading off to this time? Fortunately for me, my good grades played a role in my next adventure. The U.S. Department of Agriculture's Natural Resources Conservation Service (formally known as the Soil Conservation Service) State Office in Little Rock was hiring a group of us from UAPB for the Summer. I was headed to Texarkana, Arkansas.

I had never been to Texarkana and had no knowledge of where to live. Fortunately for me, my older brother had lived and worked for the agency in a nearby town. He and his buddy hooked me up with some of their former roommates. Now, to this day my brother and his buddy have never admitted that they were aware of what these guys did as a side gig for a living. It didn't take me long to realize he had placed me with the local drug dealers! Hello Mary Jane!

Silly me, I never felt uncomfortable in this environment. I was young and healthy, what could possibly go wrong? This would be the first real amount of trouble that I became aware of and that Jesus snatched me from, thus redirecting me from what was certain doom and a life of misery. Here's the story...

*****

With this job assignment I was in a similar office surrounding as I had been in Ortonville. In other words, the entire staff was white. Of course, each USDA agency has its own mission areas, and with the Soil Conservation Service we had to visit farmers with a much higher frequency than I did with the U.S. Fish and Wildlife Service. I was cool with this. Keep in mind, I lived on a small farm, yet I had never heard of this agency or any other federal agency, let alone had an employee visit our farm to offer us technical assistance. I was being well educated.

Just like the staff in Minnesota, everyone here was courteous and we had a great office atmosphere. While sitting at my assigned desk in the air conditioning, I would think about those hot days chopping cotton when I was younger. Needless to say, I had come up in the world. But back at the place where I roomed with three of my brother's former roommates, their activity could have caused my world to come crashing down fast! But it made for a very interesting summer.

One hot summer night around eight in the evening, my roommates asked if I wanted to go to Idabel, Oklahoma. I thought, sure, I've never been there before. Again, keep in mind that I'm very adventurous. Me and John, one of my roommates (I've changed his name to maintain his privacy) struck out! After about an hour and a half of driving we pulled into the apartment complex. I was told to wait here and keep an eye out. I thought, *Keep an eye out? For what?*

I jammed to the music on the radio. Approximately twenty minutes later, John returned with a brown paper bag. He lifted the hood, fumbled around a bit, then jumped in and we took off. Unsure of what was happening, I begin to put two and two together. But I still wanted to know for sure. I asked him, "What is that and why is it under the hood?"

He replied that it was marijuana and that if we're stopped, the cops will not think to look under the hood. Or, at least, he hoped the cops wouldn't look there.

We trucked on down the road back to Texarkana. Safely back at the crib (at least I was silly enough to think it was safe) I realized I had been on my first drug run. I couldn't wait to tell the fellas back home about this!

The summer continued without incident, although our place was becoming well known as the place to score drugs. Pills, cocaine, marijuana, you name it and the guys on that street had it. Everyone showed up. Male, female, all races. I never got involved in any of the transactions, I was simply the look-out and was given all the dope I could smoke. Not wanting to be a square, I pretended I was an old hand at it. I even tried cocaine for the first time. John had a line on the table and said, "Here snort this!"

I did.

I guess it was cut so thin I never got a buzz, therefore I never tried it again. With our growing popularity the cops were soon knocking on our door. Actually, they were kicking in the door. I was correct!

It was weird and seemed surreal. It was in the middle of a work week in the early afternoon. Two of the guys had gone to Shreveport to pick up tickets for the upcoming Commodores concert that would be happening that Friday. I was there alone with John.

Suddenly there was a knock at the door. It was three African American male customers. He invited them in. He told two of them to have a seat at the table. We were watching a movie called *Gordon's War*, a black exploitation film about pimps and drugs.

Here's where it gets even stranger.

John and one of the guys had gone back to his room to discuss business. The other two guys and I were sampling the product. We all continued to watch the movie.

In the very next scene, it was a drug bust. Police sirens screaming and cars coming from all directions. The actor's bum rushed the house and proceeded to kick in the door. At that very moment, there was a simultaneous loud bang on our door! One of the guys passing the joint said, "Man, that sounded real!" We all laughed, saying "You damn right!"

There was a second knock that did not sync with the movie.

I jumped up and asked, "Who is it?

The voice on the other side said, "It's the police. Open up."

Panicking I ran back to the back where John and his customer were and yelled, "Hey man, it's the cops!"

He had drugs spread out all over the bed. He quickly threw it back into his brown paper bag and went a short distance down the hall and stopped.

The house we lived in was old and luckily for us the floor in one spot had separated from the wall just wide enough for him to shove his stash up into the wall, which totally concealed it. By the time he stood up both the front and back door flew open. In rushed Texarkana PD!

Fortunately, they did not bring drug sniffing dogs. If they had, yours truly would have done a very long sentence in jail. All that I had worked for would have come to an immediate end.

The cops were merciless, and they destroyed the entire house. They flipped over mattresses, tossed drawers, emptied kitchen cabinets. The place was a mess. But the one place they could not have imagined to look was safe and sound. I was sweating every time a pair of shoes would walk pass that gap between the floor and wall. But, finally, they gave up.

It just so happened that John knew one of the officers. He asked him, "Bob, what is this?"

Bob replied, "We got a tip you guys are dealing in dope. You better watch yourself." As Bob and the other cops were leaving, he looked over at me and our scared-to-death customers and said, "You guys need to use an air freshener." That let us know the dope scent was overwhelming.

Whew! The providence of Jesus Christ.

After this incident, I immediately recognized that there is no glamour in being the local dope dealer. I felt more comfortable at work than at home. Every chance I got to go home to Cotton Plant for the weekend, I took it.

In addition to this rude awakening of how my life could have dramatically been altered for the worst, this was also the summer that we lost the King of Rock n Roll. I remember it like it was yesterday. Me, the District Conservationist, and the technician had been out on a survey and had just returned to the office. When we got in the Soil and Water Conservation District Secretary was crying her eyes out. The District Conservationist asked her what was the matter? She replied that Elvis had died. I was a big fan of Elvis and like millions I had watched his many specials on TV and thought he was a very cool cat. I could tell this event saddened my white colleagues. I felt their pain and was very sympathetic. This was a first. Again, God was opening my heart.

Unlike the recording artist Rick James, I never fell in love with Mary Jane. However, she would pop up in my life from time to time. Eventually this relationship ended with the overwhelming power of Jesus Christ. More about this in Chapter 4.

Memories of a Track Star: Part II

TO: Selected Track & Field Athletes from NAIA District 17

SUBJECT: NAIA District 17-National Mexican Select Team Meet

Dear Athlete:

You have been selected to represent the NAIA in track & field competition against the National Mexican Select team. The event will be held in Mexico City, Mexico on May 26-27, 1973.

Selected athletes will leave Little Rock, Ark. on Thursday, May 24 and return on Monday, May 28 or Tuesday, May 29.

Athletes that accept the invitation must obtain a travel permit. A birth certificate is needed to obtain the permit. There is no charge for this permit and it is obtained through American Airline in Little Rock or any other major city serviced by American.

Each athlete will need $5 for airport tax to leave Mexico. Housing, meals, transportation in Mexico City and travel to and from the airports will be provided.

Athletes are reminded that accident insurance is not provided for this trip. Check with your family insurance to see if you are covered should injury occur while competing in Mexico City.

We look forward to working with you on this trip. Should you make the trip you are reminded that you are representing your school, your district and the NAIA in a foreign country. We know that you will conduct yourself accordingly; any misconduct will result in the athlete being returned to the states immediately.

The following gentlemen will also be making the trip: TED LLOYD, Harding APK; JIM MACK SAWYER, Henderson State APK; BILL STEVENS, Central Arkansas; WALLY SCHWARTZ, NAIA National Office

CHAPTER 3

Jesus, Me, and the Pizza

Obviously, that summer in Texarkana was nothing for me to brag about. I was very tight lipped about my experience. I would just tell people that it was interesting to say the least and then move on to another subject.

With two summer employment opportunities under my belt with the USDA, those chopping and picking cotton days seemed to get farther and farther behind me. Moreover, my grades were great, and my track and field career was fantastic.

I probably should have mentioned this earlier, but I didn't want to interrupt my story. The summer of 1975 a significant event occurred that changed my life when I was working a job on the Farm at UAPB before the Fall semester started. This was when I met my wife. Well, not really in the flesh, I mean I saw a picture of her. Here is the story as I remember it.

*****

The university housed a group of us from various small rural towns, mainly agriculture majors. One of the guys I met, Willie Terry, was from Wheatley, Arkansas. Wheatley is approximately twenty miles from Cotton Plant, my hometown. One night Willie and another buddy of ours Nelson was sitting around the dorm room and I happened to go through Willie's wallet. He had already shown me a picture of his girlfriend, Mary Summers. As I thumbed through his pictures, I saw a gorgeous young lady wearing a black blouse and green scarf. I froze and said, "Hey man, *who is that?*"

He replied, "That's my girlfriend's sister."

My next question was about whether she had a boyfriend.

His answer was no, she did not.

"When are you going home again?" I asked.

"This weekend," he replied.

My fourth and final question was whether I could join him and be introduced to this chick? He said yes.

Lucky me!

I was incredibly nervous meeting Christine for the first time. I had to pretend I was cool, since now I was a freshman in college. We hit it off surprisingly good. I got her phone number and we began to call and write letters constantly.

My buddy Willie had a distinct advantage over me as it related to courting. He could go home every weekend, which he did as if he were married already. Because of my track and field commitments, I could not go home as frequently. This put a strain on my relationship with

Christine, but we stuck it out. I truly loved Christine. In fact, I loved her so much that in the Summer of 1978 we produced another Christine, except we named her Latisha Rene.

Now I had an important reason to graduate college and get a good job. Christine didn't know it yet, but I planned to change her last name to "Bunch." However, that wouldn't happen for a few years to come.

*****

What I loved about running the 440-yard dash was the individuality of it. I mean, it's just you, the track, and your competition. Although you could run a good leg in the relays, if the guy you hand the baton off to is having a bad day, then everything is messed up. My two heroes in the 440 are Alberto Juantorena (nicknamed "The Horse") from the Cuba '76 Olympic team and Michael Johnson, the golden track shoes from the '96 Olympics. They were two of the greatest!

To be good in that race you must maintain discipline by practicing, practicing and practicing. This was becoming an issue for some of my teammates. In fact, two brothers from New Orleans were cut from the team because they did not want to practice but go home as often as they could.

One day while waiting on the coach to pick us up behind our dorm, Lewis Hall, one of these guys, said, "Let's go on a strike. This coach is working us too hard." I stood silently by and just listened. Most of the guys agreed. One of them yelled out, "What about you, country boy?" At that very moment, the van arrived and I dashed away and got aboard. The coach asked where the rest of the guys were. I replied that they are coming. They slowly came out rolling their eyes at me.

I guess you could say I danced to the beat of my own drum. I had a goal, which was to be the best quarter miler I could be. I did not plan to break any records, just win. And I did!

In the Spring of 1978, I was approaching my twenty first birthday. I was looking forward to my next job assignment, too. I didn't know where I was headed, but I was sure it would be in an office. Man, that sounded nice. An office! Back home some of my younger brothers were still chopping cotton to make money during the summer. I felt bad for them, but I gave them encouragement. I would tell them that one day they'll get a chance to work in an office setting. They just need to work and study hard and get good grades and go off to college like I did.

One of the drawbacks of being a track athlete is when school is out you have to stay on campus to participate in NAIA (National Association Intercollegiate Athletics) meets, particularly if you qualify. That year me and four other guys qualified. As usual, this meant we would be the only students on campus and the cafeteria would be closed. This meant we would eat our meals at local restaurants in town. Coach Grant would drive us to a local restaurant for breakfast, lunch, and dinner. However, one of my teammates owned a car so sometimes he would drive his car to the restaurant. When my teammate drove his car, Coach Grant would just hand the money to one of us to pay for the meals.

One day we decided to go to the local Pizza Hut for dinner after practice. Again, normally the coach would just reach into his pocket, pull out some money, and hand it to the nearest trackster. This time he hesitated and called me over and said, "Here Bunch, you pay for the meal." I took the money and stuck it in my pocket, then we all piled into my teammate's car and headed to the Pizza Hut.

When we arrived at the restaurant, we noticed the parking lot was empty. When we entered there were no customers except us. So, we decided and placed our order. We could only see one guy up front. He took our order and went in the back to, I assumed, cook the pizzas. He brought out our drinks, which we noticed, and decided he was the only one working this joint.

Anyway, after eating our pizzas we noticed that no other customers had shown up and we saw no other employees but this one guy. He was a white guy, kind of on the heavy side and he moved real slow. I guess this is when one of my teammates got the bright idea of not paying for the pizza. He goes, "Hey, it appears that this guy is the only one working. Bunch, you keep that money and we split it. Let's just skip out. I mean, look at him. He could never catch us."

Not only was this stealing, which is a stupid idea to begin with, but it went against everything my parents had taught me. It was stupid because we are all sitting there in our track workout uniforms with the UAPB track lettering on them. This guy may be on the heavy side, but I assume his eyesight was just fine, so it wouldn't take a rocket scientist to figure out who these young African American guys are.

So, I thought this was just this one particular teammate of mine talking. Surely no one else can be this foolish. However, right away I heard "Yeah, I agree, let's skip out on paying the ticket. Lucky for me, and unfortunately for them, I had the cash and was sitting on the end. I sprung up and dashed to the front counter and called for the waiter to come out.

He came out and I paid the bill. Needless to say, my teammates were aggravated with this move. They mumbled unpleasant words about me on the way to the car. Here again is the providence of Jesus Christ. When we all piled in and the driver turned the ignition all we heard was *Click! Click!*

Oops, dead battery.

We had to get a tow and a ride back to the dorm. No, I did not say to my teammates "I told you so," but it was clearly understood that because of James Bunch's decision to pay the ticket, that kept us all out of jail and prevented what would have been a major embarrassment for the University.

Memories of a Track Star: Part III

Lions' Bunch Breaks Marks

Special to The Commercial

ITTA BENA, Mississippi — The University of Arkansas at Pine Bluff's James Bunch broke a school, meet and state record here yesterday with a time of 45.6 in the 400 meters at the Mississippi Valley State University Relays.

Bunch shattered the meet record of 48.0 set last year and also eclipsed the state and school mark of 45.6 set by the Lions' Harold Francis in the 1968 National Association of Intercollegiate Athletics final.

In the mile relay, the Lions shrugged off a dropped baton to register a 3:13.2 reading, good for second place behind MVSU's 3:11.4.

Boycott Possibility Delays Bunch's Plans

By PAUL BANTA
(of the Gazette Staff)

— McGEHEE

For three years, James Bunch had been the best quarter-miler in Arkansas. Every year he had reached the finals at the National Association of Intercollegiate Athletics Championships, twice at Arkadelphia, then once at Abilene, Tex.

Tall and thin, he looked like a good runner. With long, smooth strides, he floated through races. Strain never showed.

On April 21, 1979, running at Mississippi Valley College, the University of Arkansas at Pine Bluff senior became more than just the state's best quarter-miler.

"It was the worst day of my life," Bunch said, laughing. "I didn't feel good at that meet. I really felt I was going to do poorly. I didn't know any idea what my time would be.

"Once the gun was shot, I gave up all the feelings I thought I'd just go on and run.

"I was in lane four. I had two guys in front and two guys behind (staggered start). I passed the guys in front even before we got out of the turn. I thought maybe those guys weren't feeling well either.

"After I finished, I walked off the track. Coach Grant showed me his clock. I told him 'You started your clock late.' I didn't believe it."

Bunch had run a 45.48, breaking the 440-meter state record of 45.4 set in 1963 by UAPB's Harold Francis. But the time was more. Bunch had run one of 1979's best 400-meter times.

"Mississippi Valley had two guys who had done low 46s," UAPB track coach U.S. Grant recalled. "Delta State had one. And Billy Parmer [a UAPB senior who finished the race with a career-best 46.7] ran too. There were five quality kids in there. In fact I think the 400-pace time was 47.3.

"I timed him myself, as all coaches do. I had 45.4. I jumped the fence and went to the judges. They had three clocks in first place. Two had 45.4 and one had the same as me. They went into a huddle and gave him the average time."

Bunch's time stood as the world (as compiled by Track and Field News until after the European summer season and the World Cup at Montreal. That magazine ranked him as one of the United States' top 10 quarter-milers for 1979.

He finished second at the NAIA Championships last May at Abilene, running four-tenths of 45.5 and 46.1 with a 46.6 in the finals.

Bunch now lives at McGehee. An agriculture major with good grades, he took a job with the Soil Conservation Service last summer. He's doing something he likes, analyzing land use, advising farmers.

And for the first time in his life, the seventh of 15 children raised on a small Cotton Plant farm can live comfortably. At 22, he's started to fill out, not getting fat, but no longer string thin.

Attracted by the job opportunity, he turned down a chance to go to the World University Games at Mexico City. While other runners began to think about the 1980 Olympics, Bunch stashed aerial photos of delta farmland.

Now settled in his job, Bunch has thought of competing again, thinking about the Olympics, planning a schedule.

"I've already thought about it and what I'd do," he said recently. "It's all been in the back of my mind I miss it a whole lot really. I'm doing a few things to stay in shape. If I started [training] now, I could run by the middle of March.

"In February, I'd do endurance work and lift weights. In March I'd start a lot of speed work I'd think of doing 56.0, 49.5 for the first meet and go down from there.

"If I could, I'd attend a couple of meets — the Kansas Relays, the Texas Relays — to get a couple of [good] times and be recognized. Getting to the Trials wouldn't be any problem."

The 400-meter qualifying time for the Olympic Trials, set for June 21-29 at Eugene.

(See POLITICS on Page 6B.)

James Bunch then, at UAPB, . . .

. . . and now, working for the Soil Conservation Service at McGehee.

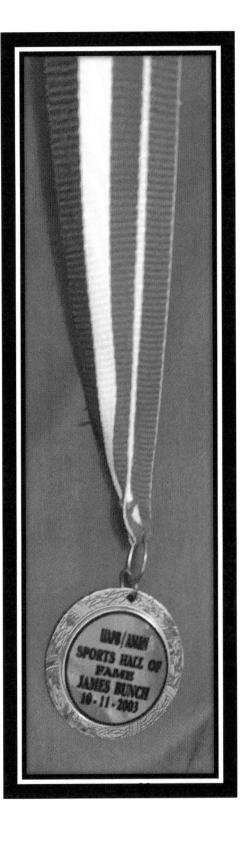

CHAPTER 4

Jesus, Me, and the Bologna Sandwich

In the Spring of 1979, I was having my best year yet. *Track and Field* magazine had me ranked as the third fastest quarter miler in the country. I had broken the Arkansas state record with a time of 45.6 seconds and was headed to my final NAIA meet. This record would stand for the next eleven years.

The final track meet was held on the campus of Prairie View A&M University. I had never won this race at this meet, but I was cautiously optimistic.

Come to your mark! Get set! And the gun goes off!

I had a great start!

As the crowd cheered, I hit the back stretch and exploded. As most tracksters would know, in an event such as the 440 there is a point when you are out front coming into the final turn and there's a weird silence where the only sounds you hear are your cleats pounding the track and your heavy breathing. At this point you know you are in the lead and stand a good chance of breaking the tape. But again, this is only for a brief moment. As I reached the final 100 meters, I began to hear the sounds of other cleats and heavy breathing. Now I started to concentrate on my form because at this point you are out of gas and often you depend upon the form. Off to my left I got a glance of my competitor from Texas Southern University in lane 4. Off to my right was his teammate.

The guy from lane 4 edged me out at the tape.

I secured a second-place finish. The winner, this guy from Texas, broke the national record. His teammate came in third. (More about him later)

After recuperating, I went over to congratulate the winner. As I approached where they were camped, I heard loud swearing. I noticed it was the guy who had just beat me. After he calmed down, I asked him what's next? He informed me he was hanging up his shoes and wouldn't put on another pair. I asked why? He said it was because he hated his coach. I thought this was weird.

After the NAIA meet in Prairie View, me and several other tracksters from different Universities in Arkansas attended an international track meet that was held in Mexico City, Mexico. We competed against their Olympic team, and we beat them in every race. If this was the best they had to offer, I felt sorry for their outcome in the upcoming Olympics.

Coach Grant picked me up at the Little Rock airport and on our ride back he informed me that I had a chance to go to Colorado Springs and train for the Olympics. However, a little country by the name of Afghanistan had been invaded by the Soviet Union and President Jimmy Carter was deciding whether the United States would participate in the Olympics. Coach Grant went on to say that I could still train for the Pan American games, which would be held later that year. I told him I would give it some thought.

By now, like the guy from Texas Southern University, I was tired of track and field. I had a baby to support and I really wanted to make some money, buy a car, my own place, and live the single life, at least for a while. I graduated and received a Bachelor of Science Degree in Agronomy. I salute Coach Levanders Randell and Coach Ulysses S. Grant for not only teaching me how to be competitive and win in track and field, but also for how to be competitive and win in life. In my opinion, out of all the colleges and universities on planet Earth there is no experience like attending an Historically Black College and University. I say to all of the graduates and future graduates: REMEMBER.

*****

In the Spring of 1979, I was offered a full time position with the USDA, NRCS and was off to McGehee, Arkansas, to start my career.

I promised myself that before I settled down and got married, I would live as a bachelor for at least one year. You see, I'm a loner and like millions of other loners, I like my own space. After growing up with all of those brothers and having to share a room with them and having roommates in college, for once and for all I wanted the freedom of my own space.

This would not be the case when I landed in McGehee. Due to the fact that I did not have a car, I had to initially find a place that was within walking distance from the office. Therefore, I rented a room from a local family. In fact, there were several individuals who rented a room at this location. This didn't last long because my food in the refrigerator kept disappearing.

I moved into a house with one guy already as an occupant. Fortunately, or unfortunately, it was on the same street as one of the local drug dealers. Hello, Mary Jane! I did not have to go far to score drugs. In addition to this criminal activity, I was introduced to adultery. My new roommate, Gary (not his real name), worked at the local papermill. His wife, however, was back home in Asheville, North Carolina. I guess you could say I was a greenhorn, a useful idiot, because I was not aware of what he was doing.

My work schedule was eight to four-thirty in the afternoon, which meant I would be home at least an hour or two before Gary. He would often tell me that they worked late hours at the mill and that if he got a call to simply say he's not here, that he's still at work. Well, these calls were every day and the voice on the other end sounded the same. But I would do as instructed by Gary.

I did not realize the game he had me participating in until one night he brought the evidence by. At this moment the phone rang, he asked if I would get it, and told me I knew the drill. Then and only then did the light bulb go on in my head. I answered the phone and proceeded to lie, only this time I was doing so knowingly. I felt bad for being a part of the deception perpetrated by this guy.

I did not discuss this with Gary. However, the next day when the phone rang and I answered and I told his wife the usual about how he's not here, for some reason I think she noticed that my usual cheerful voice was not the same. She persisted and then literally asked me if I was telling her the truth. I hesitated. At that moment Gary came through the door and I handed him the phone.

I immediately walked out of the room but could hear the tongue lashing she was giving him. After the call, he came back to my room and told me he would be back. I inquired as to where he was going. He told me that was his wife on the phone and that he had to get a couple of airline tickets for her and their two-year-old daughter. The very next day we had two more roommates. Gary's cheating days were over. At least I was dumb enough to think so. On a scale from one to ten, Gary's wife was ten. His side piece, however, was a five. Go figure.

For a while Gary would show up approximately an hour after I would get home and we would all have dinner together. This didn't last long. Soon his wife would be calling him to see what the delay was, and more often than not he wasn't in his office, so naturally there would be arguments throughout the night. I'm thinking, man, so much for living alone as a bachelor, and I've got to get out of here. Fortunately, Gary found them a place. Good riddance. My solitude did not last long because the owner of the house soon found another renter.

*****

But back to the Texas Southern University athlete who finished third in Prairie View at the NAIA meet. One afternoon I was watching the Pan American games on television, and when the 440-yard event came on, guess who won? It was the guy I had just beaten several weeks ago.

*****

Episode two involving my friend Mary Jane would be very dramatic. I mentioned that I lived on the same street as the local drug dealer, remember? Ironically, my street address was 1107 High Street. I don't want to give the impression I was a drug addict. I was a social smoker. You know, at parties, etc. Only occasionally would I fire up a joint when I was alone, like when watching a movie or something.

One Friday afternoon after work, I struck out for home. This meant I would get a chance to visit my girlfriend and daughter. The direction I would travel meant I would have to cross the Clarendon Bridge, the dreaded Clarendon Bridge. Students and others who came from the north travelling on Highway 79 know exactly what I'm talking about. Although it had been renovated and widened, it used to be a narrow stretch of bridge over water for several miles; a simple two-lane highway with guard rails, which allowed for no escape if there was trouble. In other words, there was no shoulder to pull over on.

Now my girlfriend was a great cook. And normally she would have a meal prepared for me to eat when I got there. So, I wanted to impress her by cleaning my plate. To do this I needed the munchies. Hello Mary Jane! I had my system down. Approximately thirty miles before I would reach her home in Wheatley, I would fire up a joint.

This particular night it was raining cats and dogs. When I reached the southern end of the Clarendon Bridge, everything was smooth. I was feeling mellow and starting to get the munchies. I focused on the meal I was about to eat. Suddenly I hit a large puddle of water and my car went sideways. Keep in mind, this is a narrow two-lane highway with no escape. I'm thinking *this is it*. My whole life flashed before me because I'm certain I will be hit from the side and killed instantly.

Not so fast.

It was as if a giant hand reached down, grabbed my car, and turned it straight headed north on the correct side of the road. As soon as I realized what had just happened, two cars flashed past me. Whew! Thank you, Jesus.

Needless to say, I didn't have much of an appetite that night.

*****

In October of 1980, I received an official transfer to Van Buren, Arkansas. I wound up living in a boarding house with several other guys. Unfortunately, the dope smoking continued. However, little did I know in less than a year I would drop Mary Jane once and for all.

Here's how she almost cost me my job.

As usual I was the only African American in the office. This is commonplace for me by now, so I'm used to it. The staff was great, and I enjoyed the work we did in Northwest Arkansas. One day, the district conservationist and technician (Wayne and Jerry) and I decided to go out for coffee. It was my time to drive. So we all hop into my car, which has leather seats. I started the vehicle and the technician, Jerry, remarked, "Man you sure have some strange smelling leather."

I thought to myself, "What the heck is this guy talking about? It smells okay to me."

Right away I looked down at my ashtray and saw it was opened and was full of roaches, that is, marijuana butts. I immediately slammed it shut and suggested that we roll down the windows. Wayne, my boss, replied, "Good idea."

Here is my final date with Mary Jane. It was Sunday night, early fall of 1981. My roommate's mom's newlywed was having a party. He wanted to know if I wanted to go. Sure, why not? I've got nothing else to do on a Sunday evening. He and I were the youngest ones at the party. Alcohol and marijuana flowed freely. I mean, it was all you could smoke or drink. I'd never been to a buffet like that.

Anyway, around midnight my body decided it had had enough although my eyes said differently. I started to have chest pains and sweating profusely. I'm thinking, "Man, I'm much too young to be having a heart attack."

My thoughts did not stop the pain, so I told my buddy, "Hey, I need to go to the emergency room."

I gave him the keys to my car. I don't know how we made it because he was just as high as I was. I just remember voices speaking to me and asking how much drugs did I take. Now, I'm sure I'm not the only one to have made the Lord this promise. Let's all say it together: *God, if you bring me through this I will never do it again. I promise.*

Well, needless to say, he answered my prayer and I kept my promise. I'm sixty-two years old. I have not had a marijuana cigarette in over thirty-eight years.

This was literally a life changing event. Keep in mind, I was too embarrassed to tell Christine about my hospital stay. I'm certain that I'm not the only guy that proposed over the phone. Here is how it went:

Christine: *Hello.*

James: *How are you?*

Christine: *Fine.*

James: *I have an important question for you.*

Christine: *What?*

James: *Would you like to get married?*

Christine: *What brought this on all of a sudden?*

James: *I love you and I want us to become a family.*

Just me, you, and Latisha.

Christine: (softly) *Ok.*

We were married at her mom's house on her front porch on October 11, 1981, and farewell to my dream of ever living alone for one year.

In a rush now to get out of the streets to save my life, I rented a one-bedroom furnished apartment. Actually, it was all I could afford. Tisha would have to sleep on the couch. I soon got over the thought of living alone and begin to enjoy having a wife and family to come home to after a hard day's work. Married life was the bomb. Having a helpmate was great. This meant I didn't have to cook, or at least run out for fast food, wash clothes, or clean up. It was heavenly. That is until the management left an eviction notice on our door. When I asked why, I was told because I was in violation. I had three people living there and the lease called for only two. I thought, well, just let me rent a two bedroom, I could afford it now. But they said no, none were available. This meant we had to move.

As I began to search for a two-bedroom furnished apartment, I soon realized this would be a difficult task because I only had less than thirty days. The only other option I had was to rent a two-bedroom unfurnished apartment. The key word here is "unfurnished." Therefore, I needed furniture. Not having much savings, what would I do?

I know, go to where the money is: the bank.

Since 1976, my relationship with my white brothers and sisters had evolved to a certain level of trust and comfort. I worked in a professional setting and knew how to handle myself accordingly. My bank experience would give me my first lesson about credit. I didn't have bad credit, I had little to no credit, which meant I was denied.

Now was this the true reason I was denied or was it something else? Naturally living in the south and with my life experiences, I begin to doubt the reasons I was given on a near constant basis. And after several rejections for a loan, I became frustrated and angry. I decided I was being denied because of my race. Again, I felt some hostility toward my white brothers and sisters. No, I did not hate. But I was definitely feeling some type of way.

Here is where Jesus gave me an exam and I passed it with flying colors.

I remembered it as vividly as if it were yesterday. It was a hot, sultry Saturday morning at our apartment in Fort Smith, Arkansas. Chris, Latisha, and I were watching something on television. Probably her cartoon. There was a soft knock at the door. Being the man of the house, I got up and answered it. Standing before me was a white female in shorts and a blouse. I said hello, and she says hello back. We stood there looking at each other for a second, then her very next words were, "I'm hungry."

Now one would think surely James Bunch, who has been denied the loan he most desperately needed by whites, would not entertain the thought of feeding this person. However, this was not the loving nature and teaching of Jewell and Addie Bunch, so my immediate response was to say, "Please come in. It's hot outside."

My wife invited her in as well and took her into our kitchen. We had not gone grocery shopping, which we normally do late Saturday afternoon. However, we did have some bologna and chips and a Pepsi. I asked my wife to cook her a sandwich. We engaged in small talk as Latisha continued to watch cartoons.

After she finished, she thanked us and left. Chris and I looked at each other and said, "Hmm, now that was strange." We then went back to our normal routine for the weekend.

Still needing to get a loan, buy some furniture, and find an apartment, when I got in the office Monday morning and had a few minutes, I thumbed through the yellow pages and found another bank to get an appointment to apply for that loan. I remember a white female answering and I told her what I was needing. After hearing me out she said, "I'm sorry, but I can't help you."

Immediately I'm thinking "Here we go again: discrimination." I was about to hang up, but I recalled the Bible speaks a lot about being patient. So rather than abruptly hanging up, I hesitated. Then the woman said, "I have a friend who works at another bank. Her name is Sally. Here is her number. Give her a call and tell her Mary recommended you come to her."

I stuck the information in my pocket and decided that I would take off early and go through another wild goose chase.

Later that day I entered the bank and asked for Sally. A young white female introduced herself and asked me to have a seat. I told her what I was here for and told her who recommended me. She handed me an application. I completed it as she went about her business. When finished, I handed it to her, she then scanned it slowly and said "Wait here, I must consult with my supervisor."

I had been through this procedure before and did not expect a different result. About five minutes later, she came back and said, "How would you like it? Cash or a check?"

Eureka.

"You mean I got it?" and then I think I mumbled "check" and she said "Okay, I'll be right back."

Exuberant, I left the bank with check in hand excited to tell Chris we were about to go shopping for furniture and a new apartment. I jumped into my ride and before I turned the key, it hit me. Flashback, *that white lady we fed.* Like the rushing flood waters, the words of my Lord and Savior filled me. *I stand at the door and knock...I was hungry and you fed me... what you do to the least of these you did it to me.*

My God, I just gave Jesus Christ a bologna sandwich!

*****

Standing in the middle of a cotton field as a young teenager from the deep south, I could not imagine where God would bring me. For instance, I could not see myself crossing the Atlantic Ocean and standing on the banks of the Red Sea in Massawa, Eritrea, East Africa watching my

African brothers and sisters swim and sunbathe. Also, I could not envision crossing the Pacific Ocean to Pago Pago, American Samoa, and picking fresh seaweed straight out of the ocean.

It's been nearly forty years since that sandwich. I've told only a few close friends and relatives about it. I pray now that millions read about it, and I'm certain many of you will recall the day you fed Jesus. Although I have not always done God's will, he blesses me still. One of my favorite movies is *Ben Hur*, and one of the most memorable lines I love to speak to myself is this: *There are many paths to God, my son. I hope yours will not be too difficult.*

This is my prayer to you. Take care and God bless.

Made in the USA
Middletown, DE
13 February 2023

24761213R00050